Don't Be An ASS

A Guide Book for Teenage Boys

The Do's and Don'ts of Manhood

PREFACE

Farting in class. Asking your dad if you can hot-rod the lawnmower. Acting like a goofy zombie, so the cute girl who sits next to you in math class will laugh. We get it... These are all funny things boys like to do. However, now that you're growing up sometimes you have to tone it down a little! I don't mean become a boring, old geezer - Sheesh! Just add some class to your gas.

We've made it easy, now that you've got the perfect MAN-ual to guide you, you'll never have to hear your great-aunt Edna grumble, "Don't be an IDIOT!" again.

Don't be an idiot and try to be the class clown...

That label will stick with you for the rest of your life. Let someone else be the clown.

Don't be an idiot and try to grow a beard...

You're in high school, son.
Shave what little stubble
you have and wait 5 more years.

Don't be an idiot and fart loud in class...

You have two options:
1. Lean and
lift a buttcheek

2. Have a friend
make a loud noise to distract

Don't be an idiot and think that Axe Body Spray makes up for not taking a shower before school, everyone knows, and they can smell the stank!

Don't be a sheep and do what everyone else does...

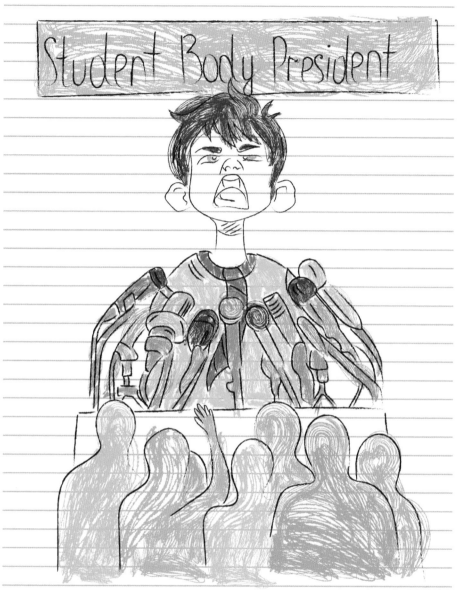

Virtually all teenagers are morons. What does that make someone who follows morons?

Don't be an idiot and get a top knot...

Teen photo album

Photos last forever, you know.

Deodorant...

Use it.

Don't be a ass and disrespect your teacher...

Be friendly to the person who gives grades out subjectively. Plus, that job is rough. No need to make it any rougher.

Don't be an idiot and pull the fire alarm...

They have video cameras
everywhere now and it will go on
your record. (This is a better job
for your idiot friend)

Don't be an idiot and forget a breath mint before a date. Your chances of ruining the first kiss are high.

Dont be an idiot and blow off your grades...

You don't want to start closing doors to options before you can shave.

Don't be an idiot and forget your manners at home...

Open the door for the girl and have her home early. You'll not only impress the girl, you'll impress her father as well!

Don't be a jack*** and celebrate too early...

See the job through and then act like you've been there before.

Don't be an idiot and let your nails grow long, otherwise you might as well paint them.

Don't be an ass and only talk about yourself on a first date. You'll have plenty of time to brag about yourself if you let her do the talking first!

Don't be an idiot and think your natural talent is enough...

It's the people with the best work ethic who make it. Push yourself to develop your talent.

Wipe until you get a ghost...

Trust me, give it an extra wipe.

Don't be an idiot and try to date multiple girls at once, they will find out and they will toilet paper your house.

Learn to control the ricochet when using a urinal...

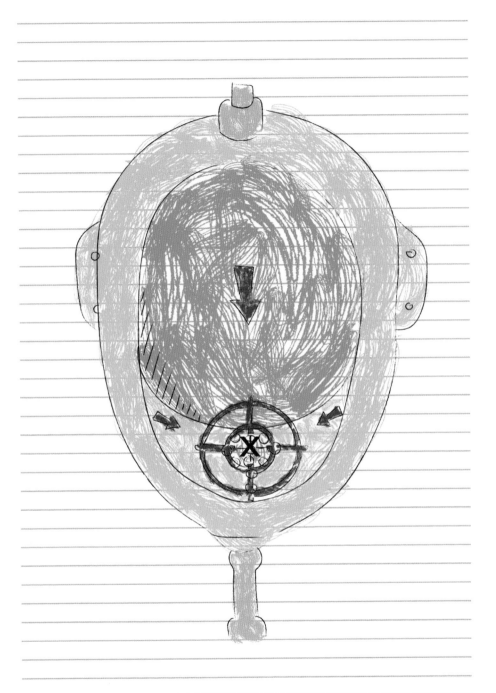

This pays off down the road.

Don't be an idiot and underestimate your oppontent...

Prepare like hell and be ready.

Don't be an idiot and think your Chris Hemsworth good looks is all you need...

Lift weights, get a haircut, dress sharp, and impress her with your personality.

Don't be an idiot and be a bad sport, that's what losers do.

Attaboy!

Mullets aren't in style no matter how many buddies tell you they are.

Looking good!

Don't put evidence of yourself breaking the law on social media, it can and will be used against you in the court of law.

wise decision!

Don't be an idiot and sag your pants, you don't look as cool as you think.

well done.

Don't be an ass and forget your
Mom's birthday...

Buy her flowers and write a handwritten note to remind her how special she is to you!

Don't be an idiot and wear your clothes multiple days in a row...

Don't be an idiot and fall asleep first at the party. Your face will become a canvas to your friends.

CHECK OUT OUR NEXT BOOK!

If you enjoyed this book, please leave a 5-star review on Amazon!